To Tracey,
Best wishes,

Beacons of Light

Nick J

"I would like to extend grateful thanks to Rob Talbot, one of the country's leading landscape photographers, who encouraged me to persist. I persisted!"

Designed, typeset, printed and published by D. W. Jones (Printers) Ltd. 1999

First edition printed in Great Britain in July 1999 by D. W. Jones (Printers) Ltd.
Empire Buildings, Beverley Street, Port Talbot SA13 1DY

Design and map by Anthony Evans
Scanning by Nicola Thompson
D. W. Jones (Printers) Ltd.

A CIP catalogue record of this book is available from the British Library.

ISBN 0 9532038 1 6

Biographical Note

Nicholas Jenkins was born in 1955 and has spent most of his 43 years living in South Wales.

He joined the Gwynfa Camera Club, Llantrisant, in 1991 and bought a (second hand) medium format camera in 1997. His son was born in 1993 and has already formed the view that photography is "boring".

He has penned two walking books, covering Gower and the Black Mountains, and is planning a third, based around the Black Mountain. Periodically he sends his wife and son postcards to remember him by.

Beacons of Light

Nick Jenkins

D. W. Jones (Printers) Limited

*For I once stood here,
on this high place,
and breathed this air.
I, too, have felt the
breath of the High Hills
on my face, and heard
Powys talking to Morgannwg
across the Ages.*

*From "Stand on Corn Du"
by Brynmor Evans*

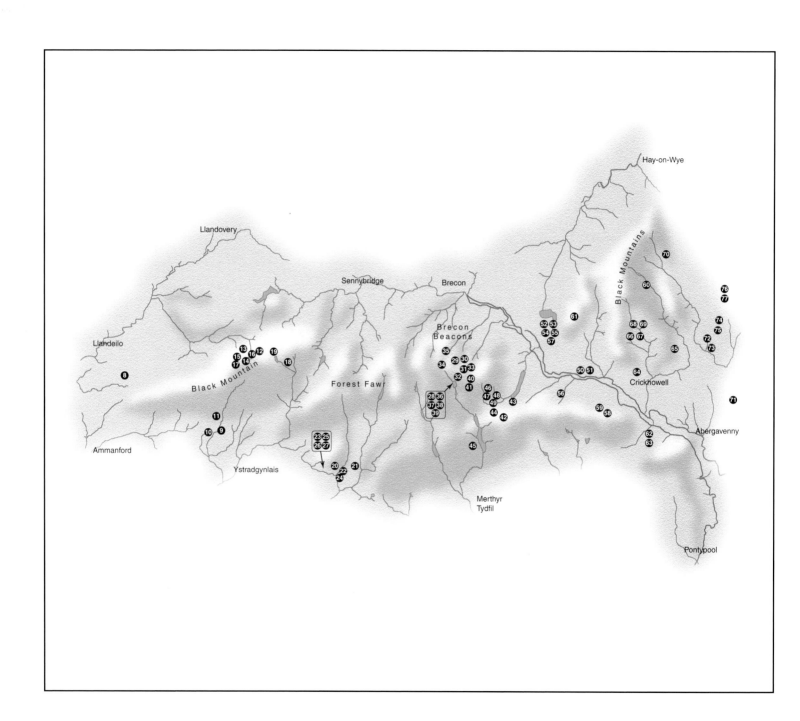

Preface

Following hard on the heels of the success of 'Three Corners of Gower', D W Jones (Printers) Ltd 'showcase' featuring the excellent photography of Peter Douglas-Jones, David Jones (the Managing Director of DWJ) was approached by a nervous but aspiring photographer. The photographer offered thousands of photographs of the Brecon Beacons for critique, in no particular order, and hoped against hope that a follow-on publication may be in the offing.

Nothing was known about the photographer when he presented his portfolio, so the odds were stacked against him. He had always yearned to see his work in print, but could he persuade DJ to show interest? Fortunately the answer was yes, and after many visits, a relationship started to click. DJ liked what he saw but felt a little refining was called for. The refining duly happened with the result that the second 'showcase' became a reality.

Being an amateur photographer, the author had the benefit of being able to plan some of the shots in this book to suit fine weather windows, and maximise the impact of the book.

It has to be said that without the confidence and support of DJ and his dedicated and professional team at D W Jones (Printers) Ltd, the dream would have remained precisely that. It didn't and the author wishes to express his profound thanks.

Beacons of Light

Ever since I was young I have always had an affinity with high or wild places. Why, I don't really know. One either feels quite at home in such an environment or distinctly unsettled. I felt quite at home. When I first met my wife, I was to discover that her brother, too, enjoyed the higher altitudes. We spent, and continue to spend, glorious days out tramping the high places of Britain.

The Brecon Beacons National Park, being almost on my doorstep, became like a second home. Hours were spent not only exploring the wide rolling tops, but also the hidden recesses and valleys in which were buried all sorts of treasures; bubbling streams, foaming cascades, green lanes and hidden pathways through natural oak and beech woodlands. I wanted to share with people the beauty I had discovered. Deep down I knew I had no true claim to discovering these treasures but they had no less an impact on me for all that. How better to share them than by taking photographs and holding slide shows? I joined a local camera club and, as if by magic, walking and photography fused.

All the photographs in this book have been taken in the period from 1995 to 1999. Some were planned and executed during a suitable weather window (few and far between), others were taken en route, as I crested a ridge or rounded a corner, awestruck by what was in front of me. I readily concede that I seek to capture the landscape as I see it, free of any vestiges of human kind. (this is not an approach condoned by my mother - "very nice dear, but there are no people in it"). If humans do succeed in creeping into view I consciously seek to place them in some sort of context. I accept walls, bridges, gates etc as being integral to the ground beneath them (the National Park is, after all, a work place for farmers every bit as it is a provider of leisure activities) but to include hordes of walkers bumping into each other would utterly destroy the feeling of wildness and remote beauty I seek to convey.

The photographs cover the whole of the National Park, from Carreg Cennen Castle in the West to the Cat's Back Ridge in the East. Broadly speaking, the sequence in the book guides you from West to East, taking in the  high windswept moorland plateaux, the 'llyns', or lakes (some created as, others adapted to, reservoirs), the wide fertile valleys and the narrow wooded gorges.

It is my aspiration, through this photographic tour, to show the National Park, not just as one may view her on a bright Summer day, but in all her moods and intimacies. Just as people may display many facets of themselves over time so does the Park, one day warm and welcoming, another day grey and hostile. From the perspective of a landscape photographer seeking to convey her many moods each day is to be savoured and captured. Not to venture out in pouring rain is to miss the magic of a shaft of sunlight striking Pen y Fan against a black and brooding sky. The Brecon Beacons National Park is a special place for me and, now, hopefully for you too.

The imposing structure of Carreg Cennen Castle. Daunting but alas not impregnable.

Waterfalls on the Afon Twrch, deep in the Black Mountain.

All that remains of the once busy Henllys Colliery, Cwm Twrch.

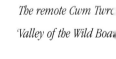

The remote Cwm Twrc 'Valley of the Wild Boa

Fan Foel from Bannau Sir Gaer, 'broadside on'.

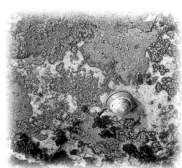

Bannau Sir Gaer, the Carmarthen Fan, (also known as Picws Du - the Black Peak) from just below Llyn y Fan Fach.

Llyn y Fan Fach from Bannau Sir Gaer; a raven's eye view.

Llyn y Fan Fach 'length on' from the heights of Tyle Gwyn.

*Llyn y Fan Fach shore -
so still you can almost
sense the presence of
'The Lady of the Lake'.*

*The tops of Bannau Sir Gaer
from Tyle Gwyn.*

Maen Mawr (the Great Stone),
off the minor mountain road
to Trecastle broods over her
twenty two smaller siblings.

The heights of Bannau Brycheiniog
reflected in Llyn y Fan Fawr, the
sense of drama heightened by the
remoteness of this wild lake.

The Afon Nedd tumbles relentlessly through the limestone belt which borders the Park to the south west.

The Afon Mellte above Sgwd y Pannwr, on a warm February day.

Sgwd Gwladys at her angriest, after several weeks of unremitting downpour.

The Horseshoe Falls on the Afon Nedd.

The Afon Nedd in

her summer finery.

Pump Pwll (the Five Pools)
foaming below Sgwd Gwladys
on the Afon Pyrddin.

25

*The waters of the Afon
Pyrddin cascading
over Sgwd Gwladys.*

Sgwd Gwlady
bordered b
midsummer green

Upper Neuadd Reservoir, lit up as only nature knows how.

Cribyn, a solitary walker alone on the ridge.

Cribyn at 5.30 am. One summer morning I was an unexpected guest as she gradually revealed herself.

*Upper Neuadd Reservoir
at dawn, from the slopes
of Fan y Big.*

*Pen y Fan
illuminated by the
last throes of winter
evening light.*

*Across Cribyn to Fan y Big -
not a day to carry a metal
tripod without gloves.*

Pen y Fan disappearing into the depths of winter.

Winter icing on Pen y Fan's cake.

The Upper Neuadd Reservoir. The stillness of an early summer morning brought its own unique light, accompanied by a squadron of midges.

Pen y Fan, on one of those special days that happen along all too infrequently.

The Upper Neuadd Reservoir in the bleak mid winter.

*Pen y Fan
mirrored in an
icy Upper Neuadd
reservoir.*

*Pen y Fan between
the beeches of Upper
Neuadd; almost a
peep show.*

The Central Beacons
on an autumn day
created for walkers.

Graig Fan Ddu from the
'Roman Road' leading
to the Cwm Cynwyn Gap.

Boundary stone near the Chwar yr Hendre quarry; the view from lying on my stomach about eighteen inches away.

Talybont Reservoir, seen end on from the ridge above the Caerfanell valley.

An un-named little stream 'discovered' above, and to the west of, Pontsticill Reservoir.

Pontsticill Reservoir bathed in early morning winter light.

Falls at Blaen y Glyn on the Afon Caerfanell.

Falls at Nant Bwrefwr, near Blaen y Glyn but rather more tucked away.

Falls above Blaen y
Glyn, taken in drizzle
under a rather lurid
golf brolly.

The upper reaches of the
Afon Caerfanell taken
after a dry spell.
Sometimes less is more.

*The River Usk and
Tor y Foel from
Llangynidyr Bridge*

*Llangynidyr Bridge.
Four hundred years old
and still looking good.*

Across Llangorse Lake
(Llyn Syfaddan) to
Mynydd Troed from
Allt yr Esgair.

Looking west up the Usk
Valley from Allt yr Esgair.

From Allt yr Esgair, over Talybont-on-Usk and on up to Waun Rydd.

Looking east down the Usk Valley from Allt yr Esgair. I was taken by the contrast between the duller green of the uncultivated upland and the vibrant green of the valley floor.

The view north west
from the 'bends' on
the Beaufort to
Llangynidyr
mountain road.

*Allt yr Esgair. There
are trees and there
are trees. This one
just took my fancy!*

Llangattock Escarpment.
A formidable limestone
scarp riddled with cave
systems of some renown.

"Mum, what's he pointing at us?"
Curious sheep on Llangattock Escarpment.

The Grwyne Fawr river at Blaen y Cwm.

From the summit of Mynydd Llangorse looking east to the tilt of Pen Allt Mawr and Pen Cerrig Calch, reminiscent of "a ship's table in a rough sea".

The peaceful
tranquility of the
Clydach Gorge,
near Gilwern.

One of a number
of streams tumbling
into the Afon
Clydach.

*The Grwyne Fechan river near
Llangenny. This scene rescued an
otherwise photographically fruitless
day up on the Sugarloaf.*

The beautifully situated medieval church of St. Issui at Partrishow, above the Grwyne Fawr valley.

Similar view to that on page 66. I was inspired!

Looking up the remote Grwyne Fechan valley. You could spend all day here and not meet another soul.

A little waterfall with a big backdrop. This is near the top of the Grwyne Fechan valley, with Waun Fach ahead and to the right.

The Grwyne Fechan valley was not always so deserted.

Darren Lwyd, from the Baptist Chapel at Capel y Ffin.

The uninterrupted view north from the summit of Ysgyryd (Skirrid) Fawr.

The hamlet of Cwmyoy,
across the Vale of Ewyas.

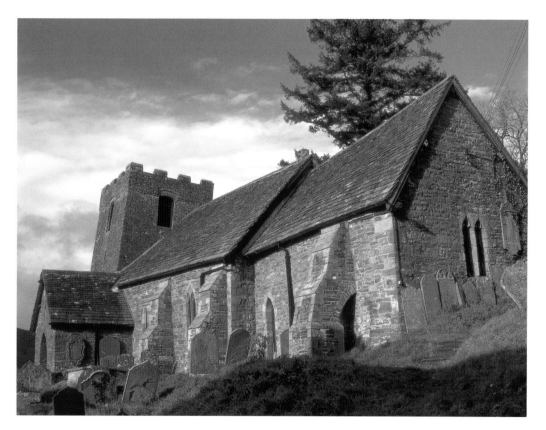

St. Martin's Church, Cwmyoy.
Built on the aftermath of a
landslide the church walls
lean in all directions!

A crisp, clear winters day on the Offa's Dyke Path, Hatterrall Hill. The hill in the background is The Skirrid.

Low winter sun on a clear day can have a magical effect. This is on the walk up to Hatterrall Hill out of Cwm Iou (Cwmyoy).

Looking down the Vale of Olchon. Shortly before
I took this I fell down the hillside and nearly
got to know the Vale on very intimate terms.

Path waymarker on
the Black Mountain.

Beacons of Light

The following notes are offered as a guide to those interested. In all cases (except where stated) film used was Fuji Velvia, rated at 50ASA. Similarly, a Benbo 2 tripod and spirit level were nearly always gainfully employed. I prefer narrow apertures for depth of field (and blurring water), the exposure time following on from this - hence the confidence of remembering f22 for the medium format shots! Gear was transported in a Lowepro Mini Trekker rucksack. I tend to leave polarising filters on the lenses, varying the turns as appropriate (the references to Polariser mean I turned the filter for the required effect). I don't take copious notes so correspondence on my offerings will not be entered into!

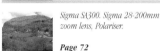

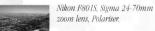

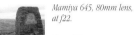